CW01433664

Original title:

Faintest Trills Beside the Faerie Cord

Copyright © 2025 Swan Charm
All rights reserved.

Author: Aron Pilviste
ISBN HARDBACK: 978-1-80559-444-4
ISBN PAPERBACK: 978-1-80559-943-2

Soft Chants from Dappled Lands

In the grove where shadows play,
Whispers dance with light of day.
Gentle breezes, soft and sweet,
Carry secrets in retreat.

Mossy carpets, green and bright,
Cradle dreams in fading light.
Chirping birds, a serenade,
Nature's choir, unafraid.

Beneath branches, old and wise,
Laughter bubbles, softly sighs.
Rippling streams, a silver thread,
Guide the wanderers ahead.

Rustling leaves, a tender kiss,
Echoes of a fleeting bliss.
Sunlight filters through the trees,
Carving paths with gentle ease.

In dappled lands where spirits roam,
Hearts find solace, a warm home.
Every step, a silent prayer,
Soft chants linger in the air.

Whims of the Whirling Leaves

Leaves dance in the autumn air,
Spinning tales of the sun's warm glare,
Whirling whispers of a fleeting past,
Embracing moments that never last.

Colors blaze in riotous cheer,
Nature's canvas, bold and clear,
Rustling softly beneath the sky,
Each flutter, a reason to sigh.

Beneath the branches, shadows play,
In this waltz, we drift away,
A gentle breeze, a whispered prayer,
All our worries lose their layer.

Twigs crackle underfoot as we roam,
Each step weaving a tale of home,
Chasing echoes of a tender time,
In the moment, we find our rhyme.

As the sun dips low, they bid goodbye,
Wrapping dreams as the day waves sigh,
In the twilight, their story weaves,
Whims of the ever-whirling leaves.

Songs of the Spirit's Embrace

In the stillness, echoes ring,
Softly humming as spirits sing,
Melodies of the heart take flight,
Guiding souls through endless night.

Weaving tales of love and grace,
In every note, a warm embrace,
Nature's choir, pure and free,
Unfolding depths of harmony.

With the dawn, a new refrain,
Awakening hearts from joy to pain,
Each whisper tells of paths we've crossed,
In the spirit's warmth, we are embossed.

Voices blend in the morning light,
Filling the world, soft and bright,
Every heart beats in a dance,
Finding solace in fleeting chance.

As twilight descends, songs turn soft,
Cocooning dreams that drift aloft,
In the silence, we learn to trace,
The songs of the spirit's embrace.

Timeless Ballads Underneath the Stars

Beneath a blanket of twinkling night,
Whispers travel, taking flight,
Tales of longing, dreams that last,
Sung in ballads from the past.

Stars shimmer with their ancient grace,
Reminding us of time and space,
Every note carved in the dark,
Guide our hearts like a gentle spark.

In the stillness, we gather near,
Sharing laughter, shedding fear,
Voices raised in a cosmic swirl,
In this dance, the universe twirls.

Echoes of laughter fill the air,
Holding memories, a precious fare,
In the night's embrace, we belong,
Together, we weave our song.

As dawn approaches, dreams take flight,
Timeless ballads fade with light,
Yet through the shadows, love will gleam,
Underneath the stars, we dream.

Breezes Carrying Ancient Chants

Winds whisper secrets from the past,
Carrying chants that gently last,
Each breath a story softly penned,
Ancestral voices that transcend.

In the fields where the wildflowers sway,
Softly speak of another day,
Echoing through the ages old,
Tales of warmth, both sweet and bold.

Breezes weave through the ancient trees,
Rustling leaves in harmonious pleas,
Calling forth the songs of yore,
As time turns, they bloom once more.

Every gust holds a lover's sigh,
Promises made beneath the sky,
With each breeze, a heartbeat shared,
Spirits dance, forever paired.

As moonlight bathes the world anew,
Ancient chants find voices true,
In the night, we hear their refrain,
Breezes carrying ancient chants.

Songs of the Wandering Wisp

In the twilight glow, we dance,
A flicker here, a fleeting chance.
Among the shadows, softly glides,
The whispering voice of night abides.

It spirals through the foggy mist,
Calling forth the stars that twist.
With every pulse, a tale unfolds,
A mystery in the dark it holds.

Through meadows wide, through forests deep,
Where secrets linger and shadows sleep.
The wisp takes flight on gentle breeze,
In harmony with rustling trees.

It sings of dreams, both lost and found,
In whispered echoes, a haunting sound.
Each note a memory, soft and bright,
That flickers once in the heart of night.

So follow, follow where it leads,
Through starlit paths and emerald reeds.
Let the glowing wanderer guide,
As we dream beneath the moonlit tide.

Dreaming Among the Birch and Boughs

Underneath the silver sky,
Birches whisper, branches lie.
In the quiet, dreams take flight,
Among the boughs, a soft delight.

Gentle breezes sway the trees,
Carrying secrets on the seas.
Crickets sing their evening tune,
While shadows dance beneath the moon.

Echoes of the day now fade,
In soft green glades, our hearts are laid.
With every sigh and tender glance,
We weave our dreams in twilight's dance.

Footsteps light on mossy floor,
Winding pathways to explore.
In the hush of night we trust,
Nature's lullaby is a must.

So close your eyes, let silence reign,
Among the birch, forget your pain.
In this moment, softly breathe,
As the woodland spirits weave.

The Cacophony of Celestial Dreams

Stars collide in cosmic play,
Whispers of the night ballet.
Nebulas paint in vibrant hues,
The harmony of dreams ensues.

Through the silence, echoes hum,
In the vastness, wonders come.
Galaxies twirl, a grand embrace,
In the void, they find their place.

Comets race with tails of light,
Illuminating the endless night.
Each twinkling bead, a tale of old,
A tapestry of dreams retold.

Asteroids woven in a thread,
Carving paths where hopes are fed.
The resonance of space and time,
In the heart, a rhythm, a rhyme.

So float among this stellar view,
Where every dream is born anew.
In the chaos, find your peace,
As the cosmos sings, may worries cease.

Nocturnal Symphonies by Flickering Light

A dance of shadows, silver bright,
Nocturnal symphonies take flight.
With gentle glows and whispers sweet,
In the dark, our hearts do meet.

The crickets' song, a soothing blend,
While fireflies twinkle, dreams transcend.
Each note, a breath, the twilight sighs,
A melody that softly lies.

Moonlight bathes the world in gold,
Unraveling tales that never grow old.
In this serenade of the night,
We find our spirits, taking flight.

Branches sway to nature's tune,
In the embrace of the quiet moon.
Every flicker, a phantom call,
Inviting wanderers, one and all.

So let us linger, hold this hour,
As magic blooms like sleeping flower.
In the symphony of night, we trust,
Forever bound, in dreams, we must.

Nightfall's Serenade of Ethereal Echoes

The moon hangs low in a velvet sky,
As stars whisper secrets, soft and shy.
Night creatures stir in shadow's embrace,
A serenade plays in this quiet space.

Whispers of wind in the swaying trees,
Carry the dreams with a gentle ease.
Fireflies dance like notes in the air,
Painting the darkness with shimmering flare.

The brook sings softly, a lullaby sweet,
As crickets join in with a rhythmic beat.
Each sound a tale from the depths of night,
Bathed in the glow of silver light.

In this stillness, time seems to freeze,
Every magic moment aims to please.
Nightfall's embrace wraps the world in peace,
In ethereal echoes, all worries cease.

The Dance of Hypnotic Echoes

In twilight's glow, the shadows swirl,
Hypnotic echoes begin to twirl.
A distant drumbeat calls from afar,
Guiding the night like a glowing star.

Whirling leaves in a moonlit trance,
Nature's rhythm leads us to dance.
The world fades into a gentle hum,
As heartbeats synchronize, we become one.

With every step, the whispers grow,
Secrets of night in a soft flow.
Fingers entwined in the cool night air,
Lost in a moment beyond compare.

Thoughts drift like clouds in a starlit sea,
Beneath the canopy, wild and free.
Echoes of laughter blend into the light,
Carried on breezes that weave through the night.

Together we sway, the world fades away,
In this hypnotic dance, we wish to stay.
Time loses meaning, we're spellbound and bold,
As the night cradles us in silence untold.

Crystalline Notes in the Canopy

Amidst the leaves, a soft note sings,
Crystalline whispers the forest brings.
Each droplet sparkles in morning's grace,
Nature's music fills every space.

A chorus of life from the branches high,
Birds join in, painting the sky.
Harmonies echo through emerald halls,
As sunlight dances, and the silence falls.

Beneath the trees, the grass is alive,
The pulse of the earth in every strive.
Rustling whispers weave a soft thread,
In this wondrous world where magic is spread.

Flowing rivers hum their ancient tunes,
Mingling with laughter of silvered moons.
Crystalline notes in the air so sweet,
Wrap us in wonder, where rhythms repeat.

Each layer of sound a tender embrace,
Inviting the heart to find its place.
In the canopy's arms, we learn to see,
The beauty of life, wild and free.

Phantom Songs of the Forgotten Wild

In the stillness where shadows play,
Phantom songs weave through the gray.
Echoes of spirits from long ago,
In whispers of dusk, their stories flow.

Forgotten woods and ancient trees,
Hold secrets and echoes lost on the breeze.
Each rustle a memory, calling us near,
To tales of the wild that once lived here.

A flicker of light in the twilight deep,
Awakens the dreams that the forest keeps.
In the embrace of nature's sighs,
We hear the allure of the timeless cries.

With every step, the past unfolds,
The stories of yore that the moonlight holds.
Faint melodies drift through the night,
Leading us gently toward the light.

In the realm of forgotten wilds we roam,
Finding in shadows a place called home.
Phantom songs linger, a haunting refrain,
In the dance of the dusk, their magic remains.

Lullabies from the Heart of Nature

Whispers of leaves in the gentle breeze,
Soft melodies dance among the trees.
A brook sings sweetly, a lullaby clear,
Nature's embrace calms every fear.

Stars twinkle softly in the night's embrace,
Moonlight blankets the hidden place.
Crickets serenade with a soothing tune,
Under the watch of the silvery moon.

Flowers sway, nodding to the song,
In the heart of nature, where we belong.
Every rustle tells a tale untold,
In the warmth of the night, our dreams unfold.

Nestled in shadows, the world breathes slow,
In the tranquil hush, our spirits grow.
The heart of nature, a sanctuary bright,
Cradles us gently in the soft twilight.

So let the lullabies fill the air,
A rhythm of peace, beyond compare.
With each breath, we find our place,
In nature's arms, a warm embrace.

The Echoing Lattice of Dreams

In the quiet hours when shadows play,
Dreams weave through the night, drifting away.
Each thought a whisper, a fleeting spark,
Painting the sky, igniting the dark.

Echoes of wishes in moonlit streams,
Flowing like rivers, reflecting our dreams.
Time bends softly in this sacred space,
Carving our hopes with delicate grace.

Voices of yesterdays linger near,
In the lattice of dreams, we shed a tear.
Each sigh a memory, each wish a flight,
Guiding us gently through the long night.

Stars call our names in the velvet sky,
We chase after visions, letting them fly.
The lattice grows stronger with each threaded seam,
Bound by the magic of our shared dream.

Awake or asleep, we dance in the light,
In the echoing lattice, our souls take flight.
Each heartbeat a promise, each breath a song,
In the weave of our dreams, we all belong.

Murmurs of the Mysterious Meadow

In the meadow's heart, shadows softly creep,
Where secrets are kept, and whispers sleep.
Wildflowers bloom with colors so bright,
Murmurs of breezes spin tales in the light.

The dance of the daisies, a gentle sway,
Invites wanderers to pause and stay.
With each rustle, a story unfolds,
In the warm golden light, beauty beholds.

Butterflies flit like jewels on the breeze,
Carrying dreams with effortless ease.
Nature's piano plays a soft tune,
Under the gaze of a friendly moon.

Each step is a treasure, a moment in time,
Lost in the rhythm, the tranquil rhyme.
In the whispers of grass, we find our peace,
In the mysterious meadow, our worries cease.

So linger a while, let your heart be free,
Join in the chorus of the singing tree.
The meadow awaits, a realm of delight,
Where murmurs of magic dance in the night.

Celestial Notes on Forgotten Trails

Along the old paths where the wildflowers grow,
Celestial notes in the twilight glow.
Memories linger like the softest sigh,
As we wander beneath the vast, deep sky.

The wind carries stories of ages gone past,
In echoes of laughter, the moments are cast.
Every step taken on this sacred ground,
Whispers of magic beautifully abound.

Stars twinkle softly, guiding our way,
As we seek the dreams where shadows play.
Lost in the silence, we find our truth,
In the celestial notes of our vibrant youth.

The trails twist and turn, revealing their song,
A harmony boundless, where we all belong.
Let's trace the forgotten, let our spirits sail,
In the dance of the night on these ancient trails.

So breathe in the wonder, let your heart feel,
The celestial notes that time cannot conceal.
In the tapestry woven with light and shade,
We find our journey, unafraid.

Aetherial Harmonies at Dusk

As daylight fades to gentle night,
The whispers rise, a soft delight.
In twilight's glow, the shadows dance,
And every sound becomes a trance.

The breeze sings low, a tender tune,
As stars awaken, bright as noon.
Their shimmering glints, a light soft-spun,
Weaves through the air, a thread begun.

Harmonies weave through leaves and skies,
Each note a secret, a sweet surprise.
The world transforms in dusky shades,
Where every echo gently fades.

In the serene embrace of dusk,
Nature holds its breath, a golden husk.
Awakening dreams in the fading light,
Aetherial notes soar into the night.

Together we sway, in stillness caught,
Lost in this melody, blissfully wrought.
For in these hours of soft repose,
The heart finds peace, where beauty flows.

The Unseen Orchestra of Eldertrees

In the forest deep, where shadows play,
Eldertrees stand, ancient and gray.
Their roots entwined, a silent pact,
Guarding secrets, a sacred act.

The wind conducts with gentle grace,
As leaves flutter in a warm embrace.
A symphony rises, soft and clear,
Each rustle whispers, all can hear.

Beneath the boughs, life stirs awake,
A hidden world, no heart can break.
Birdsong joins in joyous refrain,
Nature's orchestra, free from disdain.

Crickets chirp in rhythmic time,
Their harmony weaves a sonorous rhyme.
While shadows flicker, a dance defined,
In the stillness, solace we find.

As dusk descends, the notes entwine,
Crafting magic, pure and divine.
In every echo, a heartbeat here,
The unseen orchestra draws us near.

Murmurs of the Ethereal Realm

In a realm where whispers glide,
Murmurs of magic softly reside.
Figures gleam in the flowing mist,
Dreams entwined in a tender twist.

A tapestry woven in twilight hues,
Echoes of secrets and subtle clues.
The enchanting notes, light as a sigh,
Carried on wings that lift us high.

Glimmers dance through the subtle air,
Sparking visions beyond compare.
In every shadow, a story breathes,
In twilight's magic, the heart believes.

The gentle lull of the nightingale,
In the stillness, we set our sail.
Through veils of dusk, our spirits soar,
In the ethereal realm, we yearn for more.

Murmurs guide us to places untold,
Where every silence is rich and bold.
In whispers soft, we find our peace,
In this realm of dreams, our hearts release.

Twilight's Lullaby in Starlit Fields

In fields aglow with evening's light,
Twilight whispers, day turns night.
Stars begin to blink and smile,
As shadows stretch, we rest awhile.

The moon ascends, a silver thread,
Weaves through dreams, where hope is fed.
Each blade of grass sways to the tune,
A lullaby sung to the gentle moon.

Crickets serenade the darkening skies,
While evening's breeze softly sighs.
Nature wraps us in her embrace,
In starlit fields, we find our place.

The world fades, just for a while,
In the twilight's dance, we find our style.
Whispers carry the night's sweet call,
In harmony found, we rise and fall.

So let us linger, just a bit more,
As twilight's lullaby starts to soar.
In every note, a story we feel,
In starlit fields, our dreams reveal.

The Luminous Choir of the Night

Beneath the veil of stars so bright,
The whispers sing their sweet delight.
In harmony with spirits high,
Their voices weave a lullaby.

The moonlight drapes a silver hue,
An audience of shadows, too.
Cascading notes in gentle tides,
Where every heartbeat softly rides.

With every sigh, the night expands,
A magic born of unseen hands.
The darkness hums a vibrant tune,
Beneath the watchful, silent moon.

In the garden of dreams, they play,
As starlit paths guide sweet ballet.
Echoes dance on midnight air,
Crafting visions, bold and rare.

And as the dawn begins to creep,
The choir fades, but memories keep.
For in the heart, their songs reside,
A luminous glow that won't subside.

Songs Woven in the Fabric of Dusk

In twilight's grasp, where wonders blend,
Soft melodies begin to bend.
Threads of color intertwine,
Creating harmonies divine.

The sun dips low, a blazing globe,
As whispers weave an ancient robe.
With every note, the world takes flight,
As dreams emerge from day to night.

Fingers of light caress the ground,
In shadows deep, new magic found.
Each chord a story, rich and deep,
In twilight's lore, our wishes seep.

The canvas shifts from blue to gray,
As dusk adorns the end of day.
With lullabies of evening breeze,
The night invites us with such ease.

As stars unveil their jeweled face,
The songs of dusk embrace our space.
In every heart, the echoes ring,
A tapestry of dusk we sing.

Echoes of Mystic Murmurs in Twilight

In twilight's hush, the murmurs call,
A symphony so soft, enthrall.
Mystic whispers swirl and blend,
As nature's secrets gently send.

Amidst the trees, where shadows play,
Voices rise in an ancient way.
Each sound, a story from the past,
In reverie, our hearts hold fast.

The winding paths of dusk unfold,
With tales of wonder yet untold.
A touch of magic in the air,
Awakens dreams that linger there.

Each rustling leaf, a gentle tune,
Under the watchful silver moon.
Echoes weave through branches bare,
In twilight's glow, enchantment's flare.

As night descends, the whispers grow,
A dance of spirits in the flow.
In twilight's calm, we find our rest,
With echoes of the night, we're blessed.

Harmonies Spun from Celestial Whispers

Celestial whispers fill the night,
As stars converge in pure delight.
They weave a tapestry so fine,
In cosmic dance, their hearts align.

Galaxies hum their ancient song,
In melodies both deep and long.
With every note, a journey starts,
Unraveling the world's vast arts.

The heavens pulse, a vibrant glow,
Where secrets of the cosmos flow.
In every heartbeat, magic stirs,
As light and shadow now confer.

The wonders of the night cascade,
In vibrant hues that never fade.
A serenade from spheres above,
Entwined in threads of peace and love.

As dawn prepares to break the spell,
These harmonies in silence dwell.
A cosmic gift, forever near,
Celestial whispers that we hear.

Glistening Echoes of Forgotten Paths

In twilight's glow, shadows weave,
The whispers of dreams we believe.
Ancient stones with stories sigh,
As fading stars light the sky.

Winding trails, lost and found,
Silent tales within the ground.
Every step, a memory blooms,
In the hush where night resumes.

Footfalls soft on mossy bed,
Tracing paths that time has shed.
Glistening echoes call us near,
Through forgotten lands we steer.

Veils of mist, a dance of time,
Nature's rhythm, pure and prime.
With every turn, we seek the light,
In echoes lost, we take our flight.

So let us roam where secrets sleep,
In ancient woods, where shadows creep.
The past unfolds beneath our feet,
In glistening echoes, life's heartbeat.

Rhythms of the Enchanted Thicket

Beneath the branches, secrets stir,
The softest hum, a gentle purr.
Mossy carpets cradle the night,
Where whispers echo in soft light.

Leaves unfurl like stories told,
In rhythms warm, a magic bold.
Sprites twirl in the dancing air,
As moonbeams weave their silken hair.

Songs of crickets, sweet and clear,
Calling forth the stars to steer.
In thickets deep, the night awakes,
With every rustle, the magic quakes.

Hidden realms, where shadows play,
In enchanted woods, we stray.
Hearts in tune with nature's song,
In rhythms wild, we all belong.

So let us dance, beneath the trees,
Among the branches, in the breeze.
In every heart, the rhythms throng,
In the enchanted thicket, we are strong.

Secrets of the Woodland Spirits

Amidst the trees, where spirits sigh,
Their laughter dances, sweet and shy.
Whispers soft, on the forest floor,
Secrets waiting, forevermore.

Glimmers caught in nature's breath,
Reveal the tales beyond our death.
With every rustle, stories flow,
In the woodland's mystic glow.

Fireflies blink like stars at play,
Guiding us on our wandering way.
In the hush, their voices call,
To secrets hidden, beyond the thrall.

Through tangled roots, we find our path,
The spirits' joy, the woodland's wrath.
Each step a link to something old,
In sacred woods, the secrets unfold.

So listen close, let your heart see,
The woodland holds infinity.
In every branch, a spirit's kiss,
In secrets wrapped, we find our bliss.

The Dreamweaver's Gentle Song

In twilight's hush, the dreamer sways,
Weaving visions through shadowed rays.
A gentle song, both soft and bright,
Guides the lost through the velvet night.

Threads of silver, spun with care,
Caught in dreams, floating in air.
With every note, the heart takes flight,
Dancing softly with the night.

Whispers linger, secrets shared,
In tender dreams, we are bared.
The dreamweaver sings, so sweet and low,
Where wishes bloom, and hopes do grow.

Softly crooning, the world will fade,
In the embrace of silk and shade.
Where dreams entwine, we find our peace,
In the gentle song, our sorrows cease.

So close your eyes, let visions gleam,
In the depths of a hopeful dream.
The dreamweaver's tune, forever long,
In every heart, a gentle song.

The Echo of Leaves in Whimsical Time

In the hush of a twilight breeze,
Whispers dance among the trees.
Nostalgic laughter fills the air,
As memories weave everywhere.

Fleeting shadows flicker and spin,
Where secrets of old begin.
Glistening dreams on petals bright,
Twinkle softly in the night.

Crimson colors in twilight fade,
While nature's gentle serenade.
Rustling echoes, sweet and clear,
Call the past ever near.

Wandering paths of twilight's glow,
Underneath the stars that show.
Time encircles, dances true,
In the whispers known to few.

As night falls, the world holds still,
Sparkling wonders the heart can fill.
Each leaf a story, sung sublime,
In the echo of whimsical time.

Enchanted Overture in a Hushed Glade

Underneath the boughs of green,
Where the world feels soft and serene,
A symphony of rustles near,
Nature's music for every ear.

Mossy carpets with colors bright,
Invite the weary through the night.
A breeze stirs the velvet leaves,
Binding secrets the forest weaves.

Glow of fireflies grace the sky,
As tender voices softly sigh.
In stillness, dreams begin to gleam,
Flowing gently, like a stream.

Whispers gather with each soft note,
Carried on the breeze, they float.
The timeless waltz of day and night,
Creates an essence pure and light.

In this glade, where time stands still,
Hearts awaken, spirits thrill.
Under stars, the world feels grand,
In an overture, perfectly planned.

Serenade of Whimsy and Wonder

Dancing shadows, painted light,
In the twilight, pure delight.
A tale woven from dreams untold,
In whispers of the brave and bold.

Clouds like candy in the sky,
Invite the dreamers to fly high.
With laughter twinkling like the stars,
Echoes of joy drift near and far.

Every corner, surprise awaits,
Open hearts to wondrous fates.
Fluttering wings and softest sighs,
Bring forth magic that never dies.

In the hush, the night takes flight,
Wrapped in tones of pure delight.
A serenade both sweet and clear,
Spins the world with love and cheer.

Moonbeams sparkle, a gentle glow,
Through fields of dreams where soft winds blow.
In whimsy's arms, we find our place,
A wondrous journey we embrace.

The Enchanted Night's Timeless Melody

Stars adorn the velvet sky,
Singing softly, passing by.
A melody that calls the heart,
Weaving souls, never apart.

Gentle breezes softly hum,
In the dark, the magic comes.
Whispers weave through night's embrace,
Time stands still in the sacred space.

Each note carries a tale to tell,
Of moonlit paths, where spirits dwell.
With every flicker, joy invades,
Amidst the dreams that twilight fades.

In this hour, the world transforms,
Into a realm where fantasy warms.
With laughter bright, the shadows play,
In the enchanting night's ballet.

The timeless song, a soothing grace,
Wraps us in its sweet embrace.
As stars twinkle, hearts unite,
In the depth of the enchanted night.

Reveries Carried on Gentle Winds

Soft whispers dance in twilight's glow,
Dreams take flight where the willows bow.
Time drifts slowly like clouds at play,
Carried gently, they fade away.

A melody sings through the grassy field,
Hearts open wide, the spirit revealed.
Moments linger like the setting sun,
In the embrace where all things are one.

The breeze weaves stories of days long past,
Echoes of laughter, shadows cast.
Each sigh of the wind, a tale it tells,
Of hopes and wishes where silence dwells.

Stars awaken in the velvet night,
Dancing softly, they reveal their light.
With every breath, the world feels new,
In reveries that the wind also knew.

As dawn approaches, shadows retreat,
The song of the earth, a rhythmic beat.
Through the meadows, our spirits soar,
In gentle winds, forevermore.

Twilight's Breath Through Shimmering Leaves

As day surrenders to the night,
Whispers of magic take their flight.
Beneath the arch of sapphire skies,
Twilight breathes, where the mystery lies.

Leaves shimmer gently in fading light,
Nature hums softly in eager delight.
The world transforms in a silken breath,
In twilight's arms, we find sweet rest.

Stars shimmer bright, the moon takes its place,
Casting silver upon nature's face.
In the stillness, the heart finds peace,
A moment captured, a sweet release.

Eyes closed softly, we drift away,
Wrapped in dreams where shadows play.
In every sigh, in every glow,
Twilight's breath begins to flow.

With every whisper, the night expands,
Guiding us gently with unseen hands.
In shimmering leaves, we find our way,
Through twilight's breath, where our wishes stay.

Enchanted Harmonies Beneath the Stars

In night's embrace, the world turns gold,
Harmonies whisper, secrets untold.
Stars twinkle softly, crafting the tune,
Of dreams and legends beneath the moon.

Elves dance lightly on silvery beams,
Unraveling stories, igniting dreams.
The melodies echo through valleys deep,
Awakening the magic in sleep.

With every note, the heartbeats align,
As the sky sparkles with tales divine.
Nature responds to the lyrics of night,
Enchanted harmonies, pure and bright.

Beneath the cosmos, we gather near,
The fabric of time, crystal clear.
In every moment, our spirits blend,
Where enchanted magic shall never end.

From the hush of dusk to dawn's soft rise,
We dance in rhythms, lost in the skies.
In harmonies woven through the night air,
We're forever bound by the stars' gentle glare.

The Lilt of the Woodland Spirits

In the heart of the forest, secrets hide,
Where woodland spirits dance and glide.
With laughter echoing through the trees,
They play in rhythm with the whispering breeze.

Moss carpets the earth in shades of green,
Twinkling fairies in a sunlit sheen.
Along the brook, their voices ring clear,
In the lilt of nature, all is near.

Branches sway gently, a soft embrace,
The spirits invite us to partake in their grace.
Every rustle holds a tale of old,
Of adventures shared, and mysteries unfold.

As twilight falls, the magic ignites,
Illuminating paths beneath starry sights.
In hushed reverence, we walk the land,
Feeling the pulse of the spirits so grand.

Through the night, as shadows ignite,
The woodland lilt becomes our delight.
In unity with nature, we shall find,
The rhythm of life that forever binds.

Secrets Told by Silvered Wings

Whispers of twilight, soft and light,
Silvered wings dance through the night.
Hidden tales in shadows spill,
Secrets cloaked in night's calm thrill.

A glimmer here, a shadow there,
Stories carried on gentle air.
Moonlit paths where dreams take flight,
Silence cradles pure delight.

Each flutter sings of worlds untold,
Ancient songs in the night unfold.
Their secret language weaves and twines,
In every heart, a thrill it finds.

Through silvered wings, the truth revealed,
Nature's voice, a treasure sealed.
In quiet moments, listen near,
The whispers call, always clear.

Secrets linger in every beat,
Carried soft on wings so fleet.
Embrace the night, let stories soar,
In silvered silence, seek for more.

Ghosts of the Forest's Serenade

In the heart of woods where shadows creep,
Whispers echo, secrets deep.
Ghostly figures dance with grace,
Time forgotten, in this place.

Rustling leaves and branches sway,
Lead us to where spirits play.
Nature's choir sings so low,
Melodies of long ago.

Moonlight gleams on ancient bark,
Souls of forest haunt the dark.
With every step, the past awakes,
In this serenade, the silence breaks.

Casting shadows, the spirits roam,
In their presence, we find home.
Underneath the starry dome,
Their gentle song will guide us home.

Through the thicket, hear the call,
Every echo, a haunting thrall.
Ghosts of the forest, we revere,
In their song, we find no fear.

The Wandering Melodies of Morning Dew

Morning breaks, a gentle sigh,
Dewdrops glisten, under sky.
Each bead a note, a soft refrain,
Nature's hymn, a sweet domain.

Wandering whispers on the breeze,
Carry dreams amongst the leaves.
Melodies weave through grass so green,
Creating beauty, soft and keen.

Listen close, the dawn awakes,
Life in every breath it takes.
Sunlight dances, paints the day,
In this moment, peace will stay.

Rippling waters, laughter flows,
Every sound, a story grows.
Through wandering paths, a tune is spun,
Morning's magic has begun.

In every drop, a symphony,
Fleeting notes in harmony.
The wandering melodies we embrace,
In morning's light, we find our place.

Harmony in the Heart of Ferns

In shadows deep where ferns do grow,
Harmony whispers, soft and slow.
Leaves entwined in nature's grace,
Creating peace in this quiet space.

Underneath the canopy high,
Where gentle breezes softly sigh.
Life in layers, rich and warm,
Ferns embrace through every storm.

A symphony of green unfolds,
In every frond, a tale untold.
Nature's rhythm finds its place,
In unity, we find our grace.

Gathered here, time stands still,
Harmony flows, a soothing thrill.
In the heart where ferns reside,
Find serenity, let love guide.

Whispered dreams of earth and sky,
In this moment, we can fly.
Together, hearts and ferns align,
In harmony, our spirits shine.

The Murmur of Undergrowth Dreams

Whispers rise from mossy beds,
Where shadows play and silence treads.
Beneath the leaves, it softly sighs,
A dance of dreams beneath the skies.

The cool earth breathes, a life unseen,
In twilight hues, where green is keen.
A subtle pulse, the night unfolds,
With secrets that the forest holds.

In caverns deep, the roots entwine,
A tapestry of life divine.
Through every creak and every groan,
The murmurs weave a world unknown.

The fireflies flit, the owls awake,
In hidden paths, the wanderers take.
Each step they tread, a heart's delight,
In undergrowth, the dreams ignite.

Ethereal Chimes in Dappled Glades

Where sunlight dances on the leaves,
A melody the forest weaves.
With every breath, the breezes play,
Ethereal chimes, throughout the day.

Amidst the ferns, where shadows twine,
A song unfolds, both soft and fine.
The brook hums low, a gentle tune,
In dappled glades beneath the moon.

The lofty trees sway to the sound,
In harmony, their roots are bound.
As whispers blend with rustling air,
A symphony beyond compare.

Each note a breath, each pause a sigh,
In twilight's glow, the muses fly.
With every pulse, the wildwood sings,
In ethereal chimes, the heart takes wings.

Secrets of a Wooded Serenade

In twilight's hush, the forest speaks,
Of ancient paths and hidden peaks.
In whispers soft, the secrets blend,
A serenade that has no end.

The trees they share their wisdom grand,
With roots that stretch through fertile land.
The crickets chirp, the nightingale,
Compose a tune where dreams prevail.

The starlit skies, a velvet cloak,
Where every sigh and glance evoke.
Through rustling leaves, the stories fly,
In wooded realms, where echoes lie.

Beneath the boughs, time bends and flows,
In every breath, a love bestows.
Each note a promise, drawn from night,
In a serenade, the heart takes flight.

Melodies of the Hidden Fae

Where flowers bloom in secret glades,
The hidden fae weave serenades.
With laughter light and voices bright,
They dance beneath the silver light.

In twirls and leaps, they grace the air,
With fabrics spun from dreams laid bare.
Each petal soft, a gentle sigh,
In melodies that flutter by.

The moonlit paths, a playground wide,
Where joy and wonder unconfide.
Through whispered tales, the light they seek,
In every note, the magic speaks.

With twinkling eyes and sparkling flair,
They gather joy from everywhere.
In hidden nooks, their songs remain,
Melodies of the fae's domain.

Twinkle of Starlight in Mirthful Tunes

In the stillness of the night,
Stars twinkle with delight.
Their whispers softly play,
Mirthful tunes on display.

Dreamers drift in their glow,
Paths of silver gently flow.
Melodies sweetly blend,
As magic starts to send.

Hearts align with the skies,
In the dance where joy flies.
Each note a shimmering spark,
Guiding souls through the dark.

Laughter echoes through the air,
Carried on a breeze so rare.
With every twinkling star,
Chasing dreams, near and far.

Mirthful tunes take their flight,
In the embrace of the night.
Twinkling lights hum along,
Join the starlit song.

A Magical Waltz Through Faerie Veils

In forests deep where shadows play,
Faeries twirl and drift away.
With laughter light as morning dew,
They beckon us to gently strew.

Veils of gossamer unfold,
Whispers of enchantment told.
A dance beneath the ancient trees,
Carried by a fragrant breeze.

Moonbeams weave through leaves aglow,
Each step, a tale we long to know.
In circles spun from dreams and light,
The faeries dance into the night.

Glimmers of magic softly call,
As we sway within their thrall.
With every turn, a spell is cast,
In this waltz, we find our past.

Join the melody of the glade,
As faerie secrets serenade.
In this world of wonder's grace,
Lost in joy, we find our place.

Enigmatic Harmonies Under Moonlit Skies

Beneath the moon's soft, silver gaze,
Harmonies weave in mystic ways.
Silken whispers float on high,
As stars conspire in the sky.

Intriguing shadows dance and sway,
In the night where dreams shall play.
Each note crafted from the night,
Enigmas swirl in soft twilight.

Lunar beams in gentle touch,
Caress the world, oh so much.
As secrets weave through hidden streams,
Our hearts awaken with their dreams.

Melodies rise on the night air,
Enigmatic tunes everywhere.
Lost in the magic that entwines,
We find our voice in ancient lines.

So let us sway in moon's embrace,
In harmonies that time can't chase.
Under skies of twilight blue,
We dance to the rhythms true.

The Dance of Veils in Dappled Light

In gardens where the shadows play,
Veils of light twirl and sway.
With every gust, they softly sigh,
Dappled patterns flutter by.

Whispers fill the emerald glade,
As nature's secrets are portrayed.
A dance of colors, deep and bright,
In the gentle, fleeting light.

Petals twirl like fairy wings,
To the sound of unseen things.
Each flicker a story to tell,
In this realm where spirits dwell.

Lose yourself in the pure delight,
As the veils embrace the night.
In every swirl, a promise gleams,
The dance entangles our dreams.

With laughter ringing through the trees,
We're wrapped in magic on the breeze.
In dappled light, we cast our fate,
As veils of wonder captivate.

The Enchantment of Silver Wings

In twilight's grasp, the silver gleam,
A whispering breeze, a fleeting dream.
Soft shadows dance on earth below,
A silent song, a mystic flow.

The stars awaken, bright and clear,
With gentle wings, they draw near.
The night unfolds its tender grace,
As magic blooms in this sacred space.

A fluttering heart, the world ignites,
In silver whispers, the soul takes flight.
A realm unseen, where hopes can soar,
Embrace the night, forevermore.

Upon the breeze, our spirits glide,
In unity, we shall abide.
Through silver paths, our treasures sing,
In the enchantment of silver wings.

With every breath, the night's embrace,
Reflects the joy we now efface.
Together we weave a tapestry,
Of dreams reborn, wild and free.

Serenade of the Hidden Grove

Deep in the woods, where shadows lie,
A secret song begins to fly.
The leaves embrace the lover's tune,
Beneath the watchful eye of the moon.

Crickets chirp in harmony,
A serenade of nature's glee.
In every rustle, stories weave,
Of magic found, of hearts that believe.

The brook hums low with whispered tales,
Of ancient paths and hidden trails.
A symphony of soft delight,
Echoes through the tranquil night.

Embrace the calm, let worries fade,
In the hidden grove, our hearts parade.
With every note, the world feels whole,
As nature's balm mends the soul.

Around the bend, the lanterns glow,
Guiding us where the wild things flow.
In nature's arms, we find our way,
With serenades that softly sway.

Luminescent Hums in the Moonlight

Under the silver, tender light,
Whispers hum through the silent night.
A melody weaves through the air,
With luminescent grace, beyond compare.

The flowers sway, their petals bright,
Echoing dreams in splendid flight.
A gentle pulse, the world stands still,
As moonlit echoes begin to thrill.

Stars twinkle soft, a rhythmic beat,
As hearts awaken, swift and fleet.
In every shadow, secrets gleam,
A nocturnal dance, a vivid dream.

The nightingale sings of love's delight,
In luminescent hums that feel just right.
Wrapped in the glow, we gently roam,
In the quiet whispers that feel like home.

With every tenebrous sigh, we bind,
The essence of hope, our souls aligned.
Together we dive, into the night,
With luminescent hums that ignite.

Soft Songs of the Mystic Glade

In the heart of the woods, whispers begin,
Soft songs bubble where dreams swim.
The breeze carries laughter, sweet and light,
In the mystic glade, all feels right.

Mossy carpets cradle our feet,
With every note, the world's heartbeat.
Wrapped in the lamplight of the stars,
The universe opens, revealing its scars.

Echoes entwine with the rustling leaves,
As twilight's breath gently weaves.
In moments shared, with hearts so pure,
The songs of the glade, we attract and lure.

Where shadows play and mischief sparks,
The spirit dances, igniting the dark.
With each soft melody, we stand still,
In the mystic glade, we feel the thrill.

Let us wander, hand in hand,
Through the soft songs of this enchanted land.
As night unfolds its tender grace,
In the mystic glade, we find our place.

Threads of Enchantment in the Night

In shadows deep, the whispers weave,
Soft tales of dreams that we believe.
Moonlit patterns, silver bright,
Entangle hearts in gentle flight.

Stars above, with secrets twine,
Crimson threads in night's design.
Every sigh a magic chord,
Binding souls with a soft word.

Beneath the veil, lost time drifts,
Embers burn as spirit lifts.
Through the dark, a laughter spills,
Awakening the quiet thrills.

Glimmers dance, as shadows play,
In the night, we find our way.
Each shared glance, a mystic spark,
Guides us through the endless dark.

With every breath, the world unfurls,
A tapestry of vibrant swirls.
In every thread, a story lies,
Of love and hope beneath the skies.

Twilight's Caress of Echoing Voices

Softly sings the dusk, divine,
Where shadows meet the fading shine.
Whispers drift on twilight's breeze,
Carried high through ancient trees.

Voices linger, sweet and clear,
Calling forth what we hold dear.
Embers glow as day retreats,
In the hush, our heartbeat meets.

Every sigh, a song unspun,
As day bows down to evening's run.
Fading light wraps us in grace,
While echoes dance in time and space.

Stars emerge, a timeless choir,
Igniting dreams, igniting fire.
In this hour, we find our breath,
In twilight's arms, we meet the depth.

Harmony in shadows we trace,
Carved by night in gentle lace.
Together, lost in twilight's song,
Where our hearts will always belong.

The Sylphs' Dance Beneath the Canopy

In emerald shades where silence breathes,
Sylphs twirl 'neath the ancient leaves.
With laughter light, they flit and glide,
In every move, enchantments hide.

Their whispers weave through branches high,
A secret bond with earth and sky.
With every flutter, shadows play,
In twilight's glow, they weave the day.

Beneath the boughs, a tale unfolds,
Of magic realms and truths untold.
In every flutter, hearts ignite,
Awakening the deepest light.

They dance where sunlight breaks apart,
Painting colors on the heart.
With every step, a wish takes flight,
In the sylphs' waltz, we find delight.

A song of dreams, they softly hum,
In rhythms sweet, the night becomes.
Under the canopy they sway,
In nature's bliss, forever stay.

Chants of the Glimmering Faerie Lights

In the grove where fairies play,
Glimmering lights chase night away.
With voices soft as summer rain,
They weave their songs to break the chain.

Chants of joy in harmony rise,
Echoes drift beneath the skies.
With every note, the shadows dance,
Igniting hearts in a trance.

Through twinkling glades, they spin and glide,
Where all the wonders sweetly hide.
In every flicker, dreams take flight,
As faerie magic paints the night.

A circle formed of shimmering glow,
In their embrace, we feel the flow.
Gathering whispers of the wise,
In glimmer's warmth, our spirits rise.

With every chant, a spell is spun,
As time and space begin to run.
In faerie lights, we find our peace,
In that embrace, our hearts release.

Whispers of Enchanted Breeze

In the hush of night, a secret sigh,
Leaves rustle softly as stars drift by.
Moonlight spills like silver streams,
Nature's voice sings in tender dreams.

Winds caress the flowers' glow,
Carrying tales only they know.
Gentle whispers dance with glee,
A symphony of mystery.

Through the glades, the shadows play,
In a waltz where spirits sway.
Time stands still, as hearts embrace,
Lost in this enchanted place.

The coolness wraps like velvet night,
Guiding wanderers with its light.
Every breath, a soft caress,
Within this magic, we find rest.

Nature's secrets linger near,
In the breezes crisp and clear.
With every rustle, every breeze,
The world unfolds with perfect ease.

Echoes of Twilight Secrets

As day departs, the whispers grow,
In twilight's hold, the shadows flow.
Crickets sing their lullabies,
A tapestry of dusky skies.

Stars awaken, shyly peek,
In a world where silence speaks.
Every flicker, every gleam,
Echoes of forgotten dreams.

The moon unveils her gentle gaze,
Lighting pathways through the haze.
With each breath, the night confides,
All the truths that daylight hides.

Woodland creatures find their way,
Underneath the dusky sway.
A dance of shadows in the glade,
Where secrets whisper, unafraid.

In twilight's arms, we find our rest,
Wrapped in tales that nature's dressed.
With gentle sighs, the night takes flight,
As echoes fade into the night.

Melodies in the Sylvan Shadows

Among the trees where silence weaves,
Soft melodies float on the leaves.
The brook hums low, a soothing sound,
In this sanctuary, peace is found.

Birds trill softly, stories shared,
In their songs, there's love declared.
Rustling branches sway in time,
Nature's rhythm, pure and sublime.

Ferns embrace the morning dew,
Each droplet holds the sky's bright hue.
Sunbeams filter through the green,
Lighting places rarely seen.

Whispers glide on breezes warm,
Nature sings, a gentle charm.
Every shadow, every light,
Creates a canvas pure and bright.

The world is hushed, the moment sweet,
In the sylvan heart, our spirits meet.
Wrapped in harmonies so true,
We find our place, me and you.

Dancers of Gossamer Dreams

In twilight's grasp, the fairies twirl,
Draped in whispers, they spin and swirl.
Delicate wings catch the glow,
As secrets of moonlight softly flow.

Dancing on petals, so light and free,
They weave their magic for all to see.
Stars above hum a lullaby,
As the night stretches, time slips by.

In the glen where shadows play,
They twinkle, shimmer, then dance away.
Every flicker, a promise told,
In the twilight, dreams unfold.

The softest breeze carries their song,
In a world where we all belong.
The night embraces their gentle glee,
In the waltz of eternity.

As dawn approaches, they fade from sight,
Leaving magic in the morning light.
But in our hearts, their echoes stay,
The dancers of dreams, come what may.

Chords of the Secret Garden

In whispers soft, the petals speak,
Secrets held where shadows peek.
Beneath a veil of emerald crown,
The heart of nature, gently gown.

A breeze caresses every leaf,
While time lingers, shared in relief.
Each chord a note of verdant grace,
In this secluded, sacred place.

The blooms sway gently in the night,
Awash in soft, celestial light.
Each fragrance dances in the air,
A symphony of love laid bare.

With every step, the magic glows,
In patches where wild beauty grows.
The echoes of the past combined,
In harmony, the heart aligned.

Here time stands still, the world seems new,
As passion blends with morning dew.
In chords of life, we find our way,
Through secret gardens, we shall play.

Fables Told by Glow-Worms' Dance

In twilight's hush, the glow-worms gleam,
Their flickering lights weave a dream.
Stories told in silent flight,
Fables whisper through the night.

With every spark, a tale unfurls,
Of hidden worlds and ancient pearls.
They guide the lost with tender glow,
Through shadows deep where secrets flow.

Among the blades of soft damp grass,
Time-worn mysteries come to pass.
They weave through branches, up in air,
A dance of tales beyond compare.

Their flickering forms, a guiding sign,
Illumined paths where hearts entwine.
In nature's theater, love's embrace,
The fables dance in perfect grace.

With every flicker, hearts ignite,
As stories blend with gentle light.
The glow-worms glisten, tales resound,
In their soft dance, we are spellbound.

Where shadows dwell and dreams ignite,
The fables told by glow-worms' light,
In every spark, we find our place,
In night's embrace, a warm embrace.

A Lyrical Dance Upon the Ferns

Beneath the boughs, where whispers flow,
An ancient rhythm starts to grow.
Upon the ferns, in moonlit grace,
Life weaves a song, a soft embrace.

With every step, the echoes sing,
Of summer nights, and what they bring.
The rustling leaves, a gentle sway,
In nature's arms, we learn to play.

The stars above, a twinkling guide,
In ferns we dance, our hearts collide.
Together we twirl, both old and new,
In nature's bliss, we find what's true.

Each leaf a note, a step we take,
In harmony, our spirits wake.
With swirling vines, the world expands,
A lyrical dance, with gentle hands.

The fern's embrace, a tender grace,
Inviting us to find our place.
Under the sky, our voices rise,
In this sweet dance, life never lies.

So join the rhythm, soft and free,
In lyrical dreams, we'll find the key.
With every breath, and every turn,
The dance of ferns, a love we learn.

The Enchantment of Nature's Duet

In morning light, the chorus sings,
Of rustling leaves and whispering springs.
Birds take flight, in harmony,
Nature's song sets all things free.

The rivers flow, a gentle tune,
Beneath the bright and watchful moon.
Every ripple, a note embraced,
In nature's arms, our hearts are placed.

Amidst the trees, the breezes hum,
A symphony where life is from.
With every step on soil so rich,
The melody beckons, a soul's pitch.

The petals bloom, a bright parade,
In colors bold, no beauty fades.
Each scent released, a fleeting spark,
In nature's duet, we find our mark.

Together we walk through thickets vast,
In this enchanted song, we're cast.
With every sound, the world's a stage,
In nature's symphony, love's our gauge.

The echoes linger, soft and sweet,
In every heartbeat, nature's beat.
An endless song, forever clear,
The enchantment of nature, always near.

Secret Symphonies of Wandering Spirits

In the twilight's hush, they roam,
Whispers dance among the trees,
Echoes of a gentle home,
Carried on the evening breeze.

Lost in shadows, they entwine,
Stories told in silent sighs,
Each note woven through the pine,
Beneath the vast and starry skies.

Gentle touches, fleeting grace,
Phantom hands brush softly here,
In the night, they leave no trace,
But linger ever, ever near.

Hear the songs of those who roam,
In the moonlit fields they play,
Guiding hearts back to their home,
Where the lost have found their way.

In every dream that soars and flies,
Spirit voices softly sing,
In the depths, their melody lies,
Awakening the joy of spring.

A Ballad for the Forgotten Realms

Where shadows linger, tales unfold,
Of ancient lands and myths untold,
Whispers echo through the night,
In realms that fade from human sight.

Ghostly castles with crumbling walls,
Guard the secret of their falls,
Beneath the stars, memories gleam,
Alive within a slumbering dream.

Silhouettes of warriors brave,
Bound by honor, hearts to save,
Echoing oaths in silent breath,
In promised lands beyond the death.

The rivers flow with stories old,
Of love and loss, both brave and bold,
Time weaves its tapestry wide,
In every heart, a place to bide.

Through whispered winds, the tales revive,
In forgotten realms, they thrive,
A ballad sung, a journey grand,
In the corners of this land.

Whispering Hues of Nature's Lullaby

Beneath the weeping willow's shade,
Colors blend in dusk parade,
Softly brushing earth with grace,
Nature's art, a warm embrace.

Crimson skies and golden light,
Dancing softly into night,
Leaves that flutter, gently sway,
In the twilight's sweet ballet.

Echoes of a calming stream,
Lullabies in softest gleam,
Creatures hush as stars ignite,
Whispering hues in soft twilight.

Every breeze a lover's sigh,
Carrying dreams that flutter high,
In the hearts where silence flows,
Nature's lullaby softly grows.

So close your eyes and drift away,
To where the colors gently play,
In the arms of peace and light,
Whispering hues of day and night.

The Harmony of Hidden Places

In the valleys deep and low,
Secrets in the rivers flow,
Nature's pulse, a gentle beat,
In hidden places, magic meets.

Mountains whisper to the sky,
As the clouds drift softly by,
In the stillness, silence sings,
Of forgotten, sacred things.

Echoes of the past resound,
In the quiet, lost and found,
Voices linger in the air,
Each breath halts in reverent care.

Through the forests, shadows glide,
Where the ancient spirits hide,
Dancing leaves in soft embrace,
Creating beauty, hidden grace.

In these places, hearts will soar,
Awakening to so much more,
Harmony in every space,
In the magic of hidden place.

Ballad of the Whispering Woods

In the woods where shadows play,
Soft winds weave through night and day.
Ancient trees stand proud and tall,
Echoing the secrets of it all.

Moonlight dances on the stream,
Whispers carry like a dream.
Branches sway with gentle grace,
Nature's tune, a warm embrace.

Crickets sing their nighttime song,
Life in shadows all night long.
Rustling leaves in twilight's hush,
A world alive, a calming rush.

Footprints trace the winding paths,
Softly heard, the forest laughs.
In this place where spirits dwell,
Magic lingers, hard to quell.

So come and lose yourself in time,
Beneath the stars, so bright they shine.
In the woods where whispers weave,
Find the peace we all believe.

An Invitation to the Sylph's Dance

In twilight's glow, the fairies call,
Beneath the stars, in shadows tall.
Their laughter rings, a cheerful sound,
As petals twirl upon the ground.

The moonlit glade, a sacred space,
Where nature holds its kind embrace.
An invitation, soft and sweet,
To join their dance, a wondrous feat.

With gentle steps, the sylphs take flight,
Through the forest, into the night.
They spin and twirl around the trees,
In harmony with whispering breeze.

A melody drifts through the air,
Inviting all without a care.
So take my hand, let's join this trance,
And lose ourselves in sylvan dance.

The night unfolds in joyous cheer,
As nature sings for all to hear.
When morning breaks, we'll part our way,
But in our hearts, the night will stay.

Cadence of the Woodland Revelry

Underneath the canopy, bright,
Creatures gather, hearts alight.
With laughter ringing through the trees,
The woodland revels with the breeze.

Drums of nature thump and pound,
Echoes of joy all around.
Every breeze brings songs anew,
In the dance of green and blue.

Fireflies flicker, stars above,
A tapestry of peace and love.
Each moment wrapped in sweet delight,
Sharing magic through the night.

Voices rise in harmony,
Celebrating wild and free.
In the glow of moonlit skies,
Every spirit leaps and flies.

So gather close, don't be afraid,
This night of joy will not soon fade.
In the cadence, life entwined,
Forever in our hearts, enshrined.

Glimmers of Joywoven Whispers

In a glade where shadows play,
Softly whispers greet the day.
Glimmers of light weave through the trees,
Carried gently by the breeze.

Each twinkle holds a cherished dream,
Rippling softly like a stream.
Joywoven threads in nature's quill,
Dance like petals on the hill.

Colors burst in morning's grace,
Painting smiles on nature's face.
With every sigh of sunlit air,
A tapestry of joy laid bare.

Listen closely to the sound,
Where all life's blessings can be found.
With every heart, a story flows,
In the whispers, joy bestows.

So linger here, embrace the light,
In the woodland's soft delight.
Let each moment linger long,
In the heart where we belong.

Echoes of the Lost Sylphs

In twilight's breath, they softly dance,

Whispers of dreams in a fleeting chance.

With gossamer wings that brush the night,

They fade like shadows, lost from sight.

In the forest deep, where secrets lie,

Echoes of laughter, a gentle sigh.

They linger still in the whispered air,

Lost sylphs of lore, forever rare.

Moonlit beams on the silver stream,

Carrying fragments of forgotten dreams.

With every breeze, tales softly weave,

Of sylphs long gone, yet hard to believe.

Among the blooms, their spirits roam,

In petals bright, they find a home.

In the hearts of those who believe in light,

Lost sylphs forever, shining bright.

In shadows deep where the nightbirds call,

Their echoes linger, a spectral thrall.

In the realm of dreams, they take their flight,

The lost sylphs dance in the pale moonlight.

Harmonics of the Glimmering Grove

Beneath emerald canopies, soft and wide,

Nature sings in the heart of the tide.

With rustling leaves, a gentle embrace,

Each note a memory, time can't erase.

In glimmering glades, the sunlight weaves,

Harmonics rich, where the spirit believes.

A symphony whispered in delicate tones,

Echoing softly through ancient stones.

In the hush of the night, a melody glows,

A serenade carried on evening's throes.

With fireflies dancing, the tempo ignites,

Grove's harmonics pulse with countless lights.

Each petal a chorus, blooming in song,

Nature's orchestra, where all belong.

In silence, you'll hear the trees softly sway,

Harmonics of life guiding the way.

Stream's gentle murmur complements the sound,

Nature's heartbeat in cadence profound.

In harmony wrapped, the grove comes alive,

In this sacred space, our souls will thrive.

Songbirds of the Misty Veil

In morning's glow, they take to the air,

Songbirds chirping without a care.

Their melodies weave through the misty veil,

A symphony rich, in a soft exhale.

With wings that flutter and hearts so free,

They carry the secrets of the towering tree.

In notes that sparkle like dew on grass,

Each song a treasure, a moment to pass.

In the calm of dawn, when the world awakes,

Their dulcet tones make the stillness break.

A chorus of joy, serenading the light,

Songbirds arise, taking flight into sight.

Through hills and valleys, their music flows,

In the embrace of nature, where harmony grows.

With every melody, the heart finds peace,

In the songbird's chorus, our worries cease.

So listen closely, beneath the boughs,

Where songbirds gather, and nature bows.

In the misty veil, let your spirit sail,

With the songbirds' tunes, forever prevail.

Seraphic Whispers in the Thicket

In hidden thickets where soft winds sigh,

Seraphic whispers drift and fly.

Gentle hymns on the evening's breath,

Carrying echoes of life's sweet depth.

With rustling leaves, their secrets blend,

Messages pure that the night will send.

In twilight's glow, the spirits draw near,

Whispers of love, transcending fear.

In dusk's warm glow, they softly call,

Seraphs unseen, heard by all.

Their voices weave through the tangled wood,

A sacred bond where the heart once stood.

With shimmering light that glints and glows,

Their whispers linger where time gently slows.

In the thicket's heart, the truth is found,

Seraphic whispers, a profound sound.

So let us wander where spirits play,

In the enchanted thicket, lost in the sway.

In seraphic song, let our souls unite,

In whispers of peace, through the soft night.

Whispers of the Wildflowers' Heart

In fields of green where wildflowers sway,
Soft whispers float in the light of day.
Petals dance in the warm, sweet breeze,
A symphony sung among the trees.

Their colors blend like a painter's dream,
Nature's brush strokes in sunlit gleam.
Each flower holds a tale untold,
Of love and loss, of young and old.

Bees hum low in the golden light,
Gathering nectar, a sweet delight.
While butterflies flit on gentle wings,
In the meadow where the wild heart sings.

As twilight falls, their spirits rise,
A mosaic bright beneath the skies.
They whisper secrets to those who hear,
In the wildflowers, love draws near.

So linger longer in nature's embrace,
For wildflowers speak of life's sweet grace.
Their heart is wild, their voice is clear,
In every bloom, a memory dear.

Enigmatic Calls from the Moonlit Glade

In shadows deep where secrets dwell,
The moonlit glade casts its silver spell.
Whispers surround in the quiet night,
An enigmatic tune, soft and light.

With starlit paths that weave and wend,
Nature's magic does not end.
Each rustling leaf, a haunting call,
Echoes of dreams that rise and fall.

Owls serenade the silent trees,
A lullaby carried by the breeze.
If you listen close, the night will share,
Stories woven in the cool night air.

The glow of fireflies, a dance of bliss,
In every flicker, a fleeting kiss.
A world of wonder in shadows deep,
Where mysteries stir and secrets keep.

So wander forth beneath the stars,
In the moonlit glade, forget your scars.
For here the night reveals its heart,
In enigmatic calls, we find our part.

Enchanted Echoes of the Twilight Grove

In twilight's glow, the grove enchants,
Whispers of magic in every glance.
Leaves shimmer softly in a dance divine,
Illuminating hearts in the fading shine.

With every step, the shadows fade,
Echoes of laughter in the glade.
A symphony of crickets begins,
As day departs and the night spins.

Amid the branches, secrets lie,
Tales of the earth, the wind, the sky.
Each echo speaks of time long past,
Moments treasured, memories cast.

As stars emerge, the night wears pride,
In the grove where dreams abide.
With whispered thoughts among the trees,
The enchanted echoes float on the breeze.

So linger long where twilight meets,
In the grove, where magic greets.
Let your spirit soar, your heart revive,
In echoes of wonder, we feel alive.

Breeze-Kissed Notes of Forgotten Dreams

In gentle whispers of the morning air,
Breeze-kissed notes float everywhere.
Fragments of dreams that once held sway,
Now like whispers, they've slipped away.

The sun peeks through with a golden hand,
Touching the earth, a soft command.
With every breeze, forgotten hopes,
Awakening hearts, rekindling scopes.

Through rustling leaves, the stories sigh,
Memories drift as the moments fly.
Each note a tale of what once was,
In the stillness, we find the cause.

Though dreams may fade like the morning mist,
In the heart, they continue to exist.
Breeze-kissed whispers remind us well,
Every lost dream has a tale to tell.

So open your heart to the winds that play,
Let breeze-kissed notes guide your way.
For within the air, dreams gently weave,
In the dance of life, we learn to believe.

Whispers in the Sylvan Breeze

In the grove where shadows play,
Leaves of gold in bright array.
Gentle murmurs weave like lace,
Nature's secrets find their place.

Rays of sun with soft embrace,
Dancing winds through every space.
Branches sway, a silent tune,
Carried forth by afternoon.

Petals fall like whispered dreams,
Flowing down in silver streams.
Crickets chirp, a night's decree,
In the whispers of the spree.

Echoing through the tranquil night,
Stars above, a soft twilight.
In this haven, peace will bloom,
Wrapped in nature's gentle womb.

Here within this sylvan scene,
Hopes and wishes, pure and keen.
Breathe the magic, feel it swell,
In the heart, where silence dwells.

Echoes of Enchanted Larks

High above, the larks will sing,
Notes that flutter, joy they bring.
Echoes carried by the air,
Lessons whispered, light and fair.

In the dawn, their melodies,
Blend with rustling, swaying trees.
Songs of love and longing soar,
Waves of beauty, sweet encore.

Through the glades, their voices weave,
Tales of hope, of those who believe.
Every note, a heart's delight,
Filling souls with pure insight.

As the clouds drift gently by,
Larks remind us, dreams can fly.
In their flight, we find a spark,
Echoing through realms so dark.

Listen close, let worries cease,
In their song, find joy and peace.
Every echo, sweet and clear,
Brings the heart forever near.

Gossamer Notes of Twilight Song

As day departs, the twilight glows,
Melodies of dusk arose.
Threads of silver, soft and light,
Gossamer notes fill the night.

Stars awaken, blinking bright,
Dreams take flight in deepening night.
Humming winds through fields abound,
In this magic, peace is found.

Swaying whispers coalesce,
Crickets join in nature's rest.
Serenade of shadows play,
Echoing the close of day.

With every breath, the night does hum,
Songs of dusk, a soft strum.
In the stillness, hearts will twine,
Finding solace, pure divine.

Wrapped in dreams, we drift along,
In the hush, we hear the song.
Notes of twilight, tender, bright,
Guide us through the velvet night.

Lullabies Woven in Moonlight

In the hush of night's embrace,
Moonlight weaves a gentle grace.
Lullabies that soothe the mind,
Softly sung by winds that bind.

Stars alight in silver streams,
Cradling echoes of our dreams.
Night blooms forth in calm repose,
In this light, sweet magic flows.

Beneath the sky, a tranquil scene,
Whispers dance in a silken sheen.
Every note, a tender kiss,
Wrapped in love, we find our bliss.

As the world drifts into sleep,
Moonlit secrets softly creep.
In this glow, the heart unwinds,
Lullabies the spirit finds.

Hold this night with gentle care,
In the stillness, moments rare.
Let the moonlight guide the song,
In its arms, we all belong.

www.ingramcontent.com/pod-product-compliance
Ingram Content Group UK Ltd.
Pitfield, Milton Keynes, MK11 3LW, UK
UKHW021648160125
4146UKWH00033B/649

9 781805 599432